QUIDDITCH

A BEHIND-THE-SCENES LOOK AT
THE WIZARDING WORLD'S FAVOURITE SPORT ON FILM

by JODY REVENSON

INCREDI
BUILDS

A Division of Insight Editions, LP
San Rafael, California

INTRODUCTION

"The Bludgers are up . . . followed by the Golden Snitch.
Remember, the Snitch is worth 150 points.
The Seeker who catches the Snitch ends the game.
The Quaffle is released . . . and the game begins!"

—Lee Jordan, *Harry Potter and the Philosopher's Stone* film

Quidditch is a wizard sport played on broomsticks. The object is to score the most points by shooting a Quaffle through one of three hoops, or by catching the Golden Snitch. There are two teams composed of seven players: three Chasers, who try to score goals with the Quaffle; two Beaters, who hit two Bludger balls at the opposing team or keep Bludgers away from their own team; a Keeper, who guards the goal posts; and a Seeker, whose job it is to catch the Golden Snitch. Each goal is worth ten points, and catching the Snitch is worth 150 points, which ends the game.

RULES OF THE GAME

Chris Columbus, director of *Harry Potter and the Philosopher's Stone*, wanted Quidditch to feel like a real sport but admitted that it took him a long time to understand the rules of the game. Eventually, he had to ask for the author's assistance. "So J.K. Rowling came up with a chart for me," he remembers, "explaining the rules of Quidditch." The screenwriter for the film, Steve Kloves, also needed help, so, "she gave me a little bit of a clue in saying that she liked American basketball. That helped me understand the hoops and the Quaffles."

FIRST IN THE AIR

"Hello, and welcome to Hogwarts' first Quidditch game of the season! Today's game: Slytherin versus Gryffindor!"

—Lee Jordan, *Harry Potter and the Philosopher's Stone* film

The filmmakers eased into Quidditch in the same way Harry Potter did with his first broomstick lesson in *Harry Potter and the Philosopher's Stone*. These first scenes were filmed on location at Alnwick Castle. The actors on their brooms were attached to rigs, which were suspended from cranes. The cranes were attached to small trucks. As the trucks drove along, it looked as if the kids were actually flying.

The first character to fly on a broom was Neville Longbottom, played by actor Matthew Lewis. "It was very weird to come to work," Matthew remembers, "and to be put on a broomstick and hang in the air, but it was also very cool." However, he had a secret—he didn't like heights! Matthew knew it was important to get past his fear and ended up loving doing the stunts on his broom.

BROOMSTICKS

"That's not just a broomstick, Harry.
It's a Nimbus 2000!"

—Ron Weasley, *Harry Potter and the Philosopher's Stone* film

The prop department built a series of broomsticks that were used throughout the films, giving the players faster and better designs, and keeping up with the new models that appeared annually in the window of Diagon Alley's Quality Quidditch Supplies. To keep the brooms lightweight but strong, an aircraft-grade titanium centre was used in their construction. This was covered by mahogany wood, and then birch branches were added. The better the broom, the sleeker the branches in the "bristle head," like the improved Nimbus 2001 given to the Slytherin team by Draco Malfoy's father.

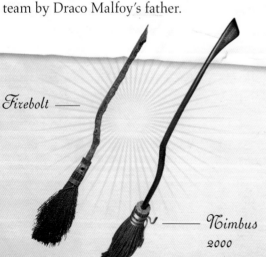

Firebolt

—— Nimbus 2000

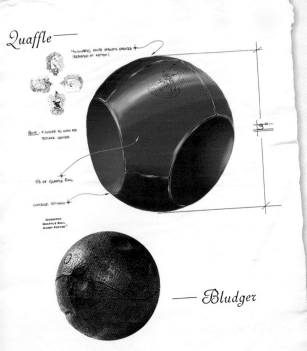

Quaffle

HOGWARDS HOUSE EMBLEMS EMBOSSED
(REPEATED AT BOTTOM)

HOME: FINISHED AS WORN RED
TEXTURED LEATHER

1/8 OF QUAFFLE BALL

CONCEALED STITCHING

QUIDDITCH
QUAFFLE BALL
HARRY POTTER™

3"

Bludger

QUAFFLES AND BLUDGERS

The Quaffle was made from a red-coloured leather wrapped over a foam core and had a Hogwarts crest logo embossed on opposite sides of the ball, though this was faded from years of use, of course! There were a total of four Quaffles made for the first film. Because Bludgers were supposed to be very heavy, special arm guards called "bays" were made to fit the players from the shoulder down to the wrist.

THE GOLDEN SNITCH

"But you are a Seeker. The only thing I want you to worry about is this . . . the Golden Snitch. You catch it before the other team's Seeker. You catch this, the game is over. You catch this, Potter, and we win."

—Oliver Wood, *Harry Potter and the Philosopher's Stone* film

A gold-plated ball the size of a walnut became the Golden Snitch on film. It was designed with thin, sail-like, fully operational mechanical wings that could retract into the grooves of the ball. Different design ideas for the Golden Snitch were tried, some with moth-shaped wings or fin-shaped rudders.

The special effects team not only helped the Snitch fly, it also created a reflection of the Snitch in Harry's glasses to make the illusion complete!

BUZZ

THUNK!

QUIDDITCH SOUNDS

Each ball used in Quidditch needed to have its own unique sound as it flew through the air. The Quaffle, the biggest ball in the game, makes a loud *thunk* when captured or hit by a player. The sound designers decided that since Bludgers are "nasty," as Gryffindor captain Oliver Wood calls them, they should sound like an angry animal. The Snitch, which is smaller and very elegant, has a hummingbird-like sound.

GRRR!

ZIP

BUZZ

ZIP

FLAP

FLYING HIGH

So just how high did the actors fly in the first films? Actor Daniel Radcliffe (Harry Potter), estimates it at about eight or nine feet in the air. In the later films, the growing actors were taken up to twice that height. First, the Quidditch players would be fastened into a harness. Then they would sit on a bicycle saddle attached to the broom (hidden under their cloaks!), and be strapped in so they couldn't fall off. Only after that would they be raised into their positions.

HANG ON

In Harry's first Quidditch game in *Harry Potter and the Philosopher's Stone*, his broom is jinxed and he falls off it to the ground. For this stunt, actor Daniel Radcliffe had to hang from a broomstick that was suspended twenty-two feet in the air. "I was wired up to the broom," Daniel explains, "with a huge airbag underneath me, and they moved me around up there. That was brilliant!"

A NOVEL COSTUME IDEA

For the first film, costume designer Judianna Makovsky and director Chris Columbus tested the outfit Harry wears in Mary GrandPré's illustration on the cover of the United States edition of the original *Philosopher's Stone* novel as the Quidditch uniform, but then decided that they needed to come up with their own approach to wizarding sportswear.

FRONT   BACK   SIDE

UNIFORMS

The costume designs for the *Harry Potter and the Philosopher's Stone* and *Harry Potter and the Chamber of Secrets* films followed a philosophy costume designer Judianna Makovsky called "scholastic wizardry." "It was a look rooted in the English school system, but it was also fantasy," says Judianna. For Quidditch, players sported their house colours and wore crewneck jumpers under a laced-up, modified version of the school robes. As the films grew darker and Quidditch play became rougher, the uniforms were redesigned to have a more modern look.

THE PITCH

Though we call it the Quidditch pitch, the game is not actually played on a pitch. "It's played in the air," says Stuart Craig, who designed the sets of the Harry Potter films. Stuart realised that having towers surround the field was the best way to take the audience up to the action. And while the towers would be dressed in the house colours of the four Hogwarts houses, the design of the arena would have the feel of a medieval tournament, inspired by the age of Hogwarts castle.

"The Quidditch pitch was so huge, we couldn't possibly fit it in any stage at the studio," says Stuart. "And it would have been expensive and inconvenient to build it in Scotland, so it became one of our first almost entirely computer-generated sets." Sections of the stadium were built for live-action shots when needed, including at least one base and lower stand as well as a tower top.

A WELL-KEPT SECRET

When James and Oliver Phelps, who play the Weasley twins, Fred and George, filmed their Quidditch sequences in *Harry Potter and the Philosopher's Stone*, they were told not to give away the secret of how the wizard sport was filmed. So instead, when asked, they would say that they were filmed on brooms while skydiving or while hanging from a rope that was hung out of the back of an airplane!

CHARACTER COMFORT

In order to make broom riding more comfortable on the third film, *Harry Potter and the Prisoner of Azkaban*, padding was added to the rear part of the Quidditch uniform's pants. Foot pedals and bicycle seats were added, which were hidden by the player's robes and were attached to the brooms. These bicycle seats were specially moulded. To do this, every actor came in, sat on their own assigned broom in the flying position, and a mould of their bottom was made and then fitted on their broom! So everybody who flew on a broomstick not only had their own broom but also their own made-to-order seat.

WELL-PRACTISED MANOEUVRES

All the moves in each Quidditch match were carefully planned out before filming began. Before the actors "rode" their broomsticks, the stunt people, headed by Greg Powell, tried out every move first to make sure it was safe. They also covered the set floor with airbags and pads, and the actors were securely strapped onto their brooms.

After the stunt team tested out the Quidditch plays, the visual effects team created an animated version of the moves of the game, known as pre-visualisation, or pre-viz. Pre-viz determines all the different elements they will have to combine in the final shot of the scene, such as the backgrounds and house towers, Bludgers, Quaffles, and the Golden Snitch. They created a list for each player's moves, which were then filmed one by one. It was an incredibly time-consuming process. A shot that featured ten players might have involved a week's worth of filming before the visual effects team could even *think* about starting work. On screen, that shot might have lasted two seconds!

SPECIAL EFFECTS WIZARDRY

The Quidditch games were filmed on an indoor set that was encircled by a blue-screen background. Each actor would be suspended in the air on a broom and would act and react while a camera filmed his or her performance. Then the visual effects team would replace the blue screen with a computer-generated background of the Quidditch pitch or the Scottish mountains, remove the blue background and "composite," or combine, the actors into the scene.

PRACTICAL BROOM FLYING

Another device used to "fly" the Quidditch players was a practical broom rig. Instead of hanging from a rigging of wires, the actor would be filmed in front of a green screen sitting on top of a tall rig arm covered in green-screen material. The arm would be manipulated by a computer programmed with all the movements needed to create the effect of flying (like tilting up or down and turning). The rider was securely strapped on, so even if the broomstick turned upside down, they wouldn't fall off. The camera would be programmed to "fly" around the actor at the same time.

ALL·WEATHER UNIFORMS

New Quidditch robes were designed for *Harry Potter and the Prisoner of Azkaban* in order to be worn during stormy weather conditions. Costume designer Jany Temime made them out of a water-resistant nylon fabric and goggles were added. She also added more stripes, and names and numbers on the back of the uniforms in the style of various Muggle sports.

THE DURMSTRANG SEEKER

Viktor Krum, a student at Durmstrang Institute, had his own specially designed broomstick for when he plays as the Seeker for the Bulgarian team in the 422nd Quidditch World Cup. It was streamlined for optimum speed, was flat on the top and had been painted with different colours on the top and bottom. Unfortunately, most of this was covered by Krum's cloak as he flew around the stadium.

WILDER STUNTS

As the films progressed, improved technology provided for bigger and wilder stunts. A wire grid system was added to the ceiling of the set that provided more horizontal, vertical and angled movements, and a more natural look to a player in—or out—of control on their broom. Computer-created digital doubles of the actors permitted actions greater than the rig's abilities, as well as for safer stunts.

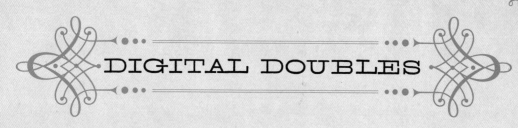

"Inside a computer, we can do just about anything," says visual effects supervisor Tim Burke. "Moves in the game that would be impossible for an actor to perform can be made by a computer-generated version of the actor." In order to create these digital doubles, the visual effects creators used a computer program called videogrammetry. First an actor would sit on a chair with four cameras pointing at him or her—two in front, one aiming low, the other one aiming high and one on each side. The actor had sixty-eight tracking markers placed on their face to record skin textures and the shape of the face. Then the computer artists worked with all the information they gathered to create a look-alike that was sometimes so realistic they would get confused as to whether they were looking at a live actor or a digital double!

Technological advances during the making of the later films made it possible for Quidditch to be more exciting than ever. For *Harry Potter and the Half Blood Prince*, the players' cloaks were added in by the computer after filming was completed in what is called post-production. The cloaks were made to flap and whip around and usually appeared to be streaming behind the players, adding to the effect of speed.

SNITCH SNATCHER!

In a scene that was cut from the final version of *Harry Potter and the Prisoner of Azkaban*, Fred and George Weasley play a board game called *Snitch Snatcher!* designed by graphic designers Miraphora Mina and Eduardo Lima. The game features a cardboard miniature of the Hogwarts Quidditch pitch complete with broomstick-flying players and models of the spectators' stands for all four houses.

TRYING OUT FOR THE TEAM

"Just because you made the team last year does not guarantee you a spot this year. Is that clear?"

—Harry Potter, *Harry Potter and the Half-Blood Prince* film

Quidditch tryouts and training were the focus in *Harry Potter and the Half-Blood Prince*, so a warm-up type suit that was simpler and lighter was designed. The numbers on the player's uniform now indicated their specific position: a Beater, a Seeker or a Keeper. For tryouts, you'd put on the suit with the number of the position you wanted to play.

SUPER·DELUXE QUIDDITCH

Prior to Ron Weasley's Quidditch debut in *Harry Potter and the Half-Blood Prince*, the tryouts and practice matches for the Gryffindor team were not seen. Production designer Stuart Craig gave the stadium a different look for those. "For the trials and for practice," he says, "they wouldn't have all the colourful fabric. So we changed it to a simple wood form." For the actual games, Craig redesigned the stadium again. The mountainous Scottish backdrop was brought closer, and the towers were heightened and more of them added, which forced the towers closer together. "By adding more towers," Craig explains, "there were more opportunities for weaving in and out of them and more things whizzing by to give a greater sense of speed. This is what I call super-deluxe Quidditch!"

WHAT SIZE UNIFORM?

"Really? Strapping guy like you? You've got more of a Beater's build, don't you think? Keepers need to be quick, agile."

"I like my chances."

— Ron Weasley and Cormac McLaggen,
Harry Potter and the Half-Blood Prince film

In *Harry Potter and the Half-Blood Prince,* Ron Weasley tries out for the Gryffindor team. Actors Rupert Grint (Ron Weasley) and Freddie Stroma (Cormac McLaggen) as the two wannabe Gryffindor Keepers are roughly the same size, but the filmmakers wanted Ron's competition to appear bigger. So Freddie's shoulder guards were scaled up and extra panels were added to the front and back of his uniform to make him seem larger. Ron's uniform was constructed on the small side, with a hat and pads that were undersized. Sandpaper was used to scuff up the leather and laces on the guards so that it all looked like another Weasley hand-me-down.

FIRE AT RON!

When Ron Weasley tries out for the Quidditch team in *Harry Potter and the Half-Blood Prince*, director David Yates wanted to make sure that actor Rupert Grint would seem naturally untalented at first. "Rupert was filmed from a variety of angles," explains second unit director Stephen Woolfenden, "and we would do things like fire twenty Quaffles at a time at him. Rupert's real responses to everything flying at him at once made for some very funny reactions, and the improvised nature of it also made it easier for him to look as though he was not in control."

FOR THE FANS

For *Harry Potter and the Half-Blood Prince*, fan-wear was created for the first time for the non-playing students to support their teams. These were "branded" with the Hogwarts name on the back and its seal on the front. The track-style T-shirts and hooded sweatshirts were manufactured in one of the four house colours, to be worn with tracksuit bottoms in grey (for the Gryffindor supporters) or black (for Slytherin fans). Luna Lovegood had her own unique way of cheering her team, of course. Her Gryffindor-supporting lion hat went through several iterations before the filmmakers settled on the final design.

FLYING CAMERAS

In *Harry Potter and the Half-Blood Prince,* the visual effects team wanted to create the sense that the Quidditch game was being filmed just as a Muggle sport would be, with multiple moving camera angles including a flying cameraman. To help enhance that illusion, the snow that fell during the match appeared to hit the camera lens as it followed the action.

STUNTWORK

"Rough game, Quidditch."

"Brutal. But no one's died in years!"

—Fred and George Weasley,
Harry Potter and the Philosopher's Stone film

For the Quidditch tryouts in *Harry Potter and the Half-Blood Prince,* the stunt team experimented with different moves to create slapstick and comedic elements. There were bangs, crashes, falls and other stunts that became reference for live-action moves or moves created on the computer. An entire day was spent dragging young stuntmen and y stuntwomen through a mud-soaked Quidditch pitch. The stunt people loved it, but the costume department didn't—they had to clean all the costumes!

THE GRYFFINDOR CHASER

Ginny Weasley, played by actress Bonnie Wright, got her chance to really show her stuff on the Gryffindor Quidditch team in *Harry Potter and the Half-Blood Prince*. This was the first time Bonnie performed stunts on a broom. "We were up ten to twenty feet," she explains, "which is not as high up as they are in a real game of Quidditch, but it was quite demanding. They turn you around and make you go fast and spin. It was a lot of fun!"

DAUNTING DRILLS

Quidditch is quite hard," actor Rupert Grint (Ron Weasley) says. "I was surprised at how physical it is. We had to do quite a bit of training on a trampoline, flips and stuff, which was actually quite scary."

But fellow actor Daniel Radcliffe praises Rupert's performance: "Ron's scenes on the broomstick were absolutely brilliant!

"Weasley! Weasley! Weasley!"
—Quidditch crowd, *Harry Potter and the Half-Blood Prince* film

MAKE IT YOUR OWN

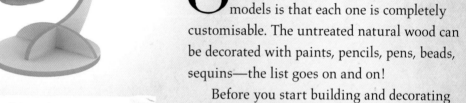

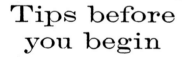

Tips before you begin

* As a general rule of thumb, you'll want to use pens and pencils *before* building the model and paints *after* building the model.

* When making a replica, it's always good to study an actual image of what you are trying to copy. Look closely at details and brainstorm how you can recreate them.

One of the great things about IncrediBuilds models is that each one is completely customisable. The untreated natural wood can be decorated with paints, pencils, pens, beads, sequins—the list goes on and on!

Before you start building and decorating your model though, read through the included instruction sheet so you understand how all the pieces come together. Then, choose a theme and make a plan. Do you want to make an exact replica of the Golden Snitch or something completely wacky? What about designing the Golden Snitch to represent your favourite Hogwarts house? The choice is yours! Here is an example to get you started.

PAINTING THE GOLDEN SNITCH

ONE OF THE EASIEST WAYS TO DECORATE THE GOLDEN SNITCH MODEL IS TO PAINT IT AFTER BUILDING IT.

1 To make a traditional Golden Snitch for display, use a good gold acrylic paint. Make sure it's nice and bright! *Then, after step 11 in the instructions,* paint the main sphere using a wide flat brush. Lay down thin, even coats of paint so the detail of the Golden Snitch model remains intact. Don't forget to paint around the open holes where the wings and the stand will go!

2 While the sphere dries, paint the wings. Again, thin coats are the best to let the grooves in the wings shine through. But *don't* paint the tabs on the end of the wings.

3 After the wings and the main sphere are dry, *continue with steps 13 and 14 on your instruction sheet.*

4 Finally, it's time to decorate the stand. Make sure the stand is fully assembled but not yet attached to the Golden Snitch. A neutral color that makes the gold of the Golden Snitch pop out was used here. Just like on the wings, don't paint the little tab on the stand.

5 *Now follow steps 14–16 on your instruction sheet.* You're done! A lovely Golden Snitch.

IncrediBuilds™
A Division of Insight Editions LP
PO Box 3088
San Rafael, CA 94912
www.insighteditions.com

 Find us on Facebook: www.facebook.com/InsightEditions
 Follow us on Twitter: @insighteditions

Published originally by Insight Editions, San Rafael, California,
in 2016. No part of this book may be reproduced in any form
without written permission from the publisher.

ISBN: 978-1-68298-006-4

Publisher: Raoul Goff
Art Director: Chrissy Kwasnik
Designer: Ashley Quackenbush
Executive Editor: Vanessa Lopez
Project Editor: Greg Solano
Production Editor: Elaine Ou
Production Manager: Thomas Chung
Production Coordinator: Sam Taylor
Model Designer: Cuiling Ke

Insight Editions would like to thank Melanie Swartz,
Elaine Piechowski, Ashley Bol, Margo Guffin, George Valdiviez,
Kevin Morris, and Victoria Selover.

Manufactured in China

iSeek Ltd, 1A Stairbridge Court, Bolney Grange Business Park,
Haywards Heath, RH17 5PA, UK